The Wisdom of

Wallace D. Wattles III

Including:

The Science of Mind

The Road to Power

AND

Your Invisible Power

The Science of Mind

Wallace D. Wattles

Mind: What is It?

Life and Organisms

Two important questions are to be discussed in this book: First. Is mind the result of physical function? And second, can mind exist apart from physical function? These are fundamental, and must be settled before we can have a scientific basis for mental healing, or for a constructive psychology of any kind. If mind is the result of functional action, then it would seem to logically follow that to control mind we must control functional action; to create mind we must create functional action, and to change mind we must change functional action. And if mind or intelligence cannot exist apart from functional action (physical) it is useless to hope for a continued existence after physical death, when all functioning of the material body necessarily ceases.

The first thing I notice in intelligence is that it appears to be necessarily and inherently associated with life. I do not find any intelligence in the realms of matter or force apart from life; and careful observation leads me to the conclusion that while there appears to be life without intelligence, there is nowhere any intelligence without life. There are certain conditions under which life is non-intelligent; there are certain other conditions under which it becomes sentient and intelligent; is intelligence the result of conditions, or is it an inherent property of all life, but manifested only under certain conditions?

Life is a force; a form of energy. It is as distinct and separate a form of energy as electricity or heat. It performs work, and anything which performs work is a force. It is well to make this point absolutely clear: the energy of the body is not electricity; it is not heat; it is not any of the known forms of material force; it is vital power, or life. Life differs from all other forms of energy in that it appears to be an exception to the universal law of the correlation of forces - if there is such a law. Heat, light and electricity are convertible, each into the others; but while all of them may be necessary to make conditions for life, none of them are convertible into life. We cannot make life out of heat, light or electricity, or by any known combination of the three with each other or with other forces. Life only comes from life. Every living being came from a germ, which contained life. The life which is today is only a continuation of that which was yesterday.

It does not appear that life is ever spontaneously generated, or originates from accidental or purposeful combinations of other forces. It is not demonstrable that life ever began where there was none before; and it is not demonstrable that any new life has ever been produced. We only find life in living organisms; but life is not produced by the organisms. If the life were produced by the organism, then the organism must exist before the life. A machine cannot generate power until it is constructed, and reasonably perfect in all its parts. If the tree produced its own life, then the tree would have to exist first without life; then it would start into action and produce life, as a dynamo produces electricity. There is no organism in the seed; but there is life there, and life produces the tree. There is no organism in the egg, but there is life there, and the life produces the chicken. The tree does not generate life; life makes the tree. Organisms do not generate life; life creates organisms. Organisms are not created perfect, in order that they may start functioning and generate life; life is before functional action; it is the cause, not the result of function. The organism does not live because certain processes are going on within it; but these processes are going on within it because it is alive. I have shown in a preceding series of articles that living things do not create life, but that they receive it, or are recharged with it in sleep.

Do those organisms which manifest intelligence generate it, or do they receive it? Is mind the result of functional action? To believe that it is necessitates the acceptance of an unthinkable proposition. If this theory be true, there must be a definite line upon crossing which unconscious force becomes conscious force; a point where that which is dead becomes alive. This is inconceivable; we cannot think of electricity or heat as suddenly becoming intelligent, and capable of thought. Try to imagine an electric current as thinking and planning its own course, and you will understand the difficulty of accepting the materialistic idea of the origin of thought. If thought requires effort - the expenditure of force - and we know that it does, then that which thinks is a *force*; but what force? And when did the force begin to think, and what changed it from an unthinking force to a thinking one? As to the expenditure of energy in the process of thought, the evidence is conclusive.

We are conscious of continuous and sustained effort in thought, as much so as in physical labor, and often more. In fact, many people who are not physically lazy shrink from the tremendous effort required to think consecutively on any subject. We *know* that we expend force in thinking, by the effort required, and by the subsequent exhaustion; and also, there are certain phenomena which seem to prove conclusively that thought has an impelling force behind it. Thought could not "go" or be transferred without force; telepathy without the expenditure of power would be contrary to all known laws of energy. Marconi cannot send a wireless impulse without using power; neither can a thought impulse be transmitted without the use of power. The thing which thinks, therefore, is a power; is it a power which *was* an unthinking power, and became a thinking one, or was it always a thinking intelligence?

Now, if thought be the result of function, then the force which causes function is the force which thinks, but it does not think; it blindly causes functional action, which results in thought. There can be no intelligence before functional action; the cause must always precede the effect. It must logically follow that intelligence cannot change, check, control or govern functional action, for it is manifestly impossible that the effect should control the cause. Does thought ever, under any conditions, control function in the human body? If so, it cannot be produced by that which it controls. Furthermore, if thought is the result of processes which are directed by an unthinking power, it is hard to understand how thought itself can be intelligently directed. If the power which thinks is not a thinking power, whence comes the ability to think coherently and with sustained effort on any proposition? Why do not our thoughts change with each change in the contents of the stomach?

Ingersoll said: "There is a wonderful chemistry by which a piece of bread becomes thought." If that were true, a change in the chemical condition of the stomach should produce a corresponding change in thought; a meat eater should think differently from a vegetarian, and all meat eaters should think substantially the same thoughts. I am aware that some attempts have been made to prove that this is the case; but I do not think that the evidence so far advanced is conclusive; not more so than the evidence tending to prove the old saying that if one ate mince pie before going to bed he would see his grandmother's ghost. If thought were the result of physical function, would it not necessarily be true that all persons whose functions were alike, who followed the same avocation, and were under the same general conditions would think the same general thoughts?

I am aware that some "scientific" socialists have undertaken to prove this also; going almost to the extent of declaring that if they only know what sort of machine the man works with, they can deduce therefrom the prayer he teaches his children at night. In spite of the profound arguments for this theory, however, the fact remains that we have workingmen who think like capitalists, and capitalists who think like workingmen; we have lawyers (sometimes) who think like saints, and clergymen who think like the devil. The immense diversity in the character of the thoughts of different men, under substantially the same physical conditions, militates against the idea that thought is the result of functional action, caused by an unthinking force. In the next installment we shall consider whether the brain can produce thought by functional action and whether mind itself can possibly be the result of the action of the brain, or the combined action of all the physical organs.

Beginning to Think

In so far as his belief concerning the origin of mind is concerned, every man must be either a materialist or a spiritualist - that is, he must believe that the human mind is produced by bringing unthinking matter into certain states and conditions, or that it is an independent entity, existing as a thinking organism, apart from the gross forms of matter which are perceptible by the material senses. In a rational study of psychology we must accept one or the other of two fundamental statements viz.: First. Mind is produced by the functional action of the body. Second. Mind is an independent entity, not produced by the body.

In this article, I propose to answer the question: Is mind the result of functional action?

If it is, there must be a definite line upon crossing which unconscious force becomes conscious force; a point where that which cannot think begins to think. There must be a point where an unintelligent and blind material force becomes an intelligent and self-directing force. This is inconceivable; try to imagine an electric current as suddenly beginning to think and plan its own course, and you will begin to comprehend the difficulty of accepting the materialistic theory of the origin of thought. We have a right to demand of the materialist that he shall show us the exact point at which the unthinking force begins to think.

For, unquestionably, it is a *force* which thinks. We know that thought requires the expenditure of energy; we are conscious of continuous and sustained effort in thought; as much so as in physical labor, and often more so. In fact, many people who are not physically lazy, shrink from the tremendous and continued effort required to think consecutively on any subject. We know by the effort required, and by the subsequent exhaustion, that energy is expended in thought, and there are other phenomena which prove that thought has an impelling power behind it. Telepathy is an accepted fact in nature, and telepathy would be impossible unless there was an impelling power, or a projecting power, behind the thought. Marconi cannot send a wireless telegram without using power, nor can a thought be telepathed without the use of power. The thing which thinks, therefore, is a power; is it an unthinking power which suddenly becomes a thinking one, and if so, when, why and how does it begin to think?

Now, if thought is a functioning of the brain, then the force which causes functional action is the force which thinks; but this force does not think; it blindly causes functional action, which results in thought. There can be no intelligence before functional action; and it must be impossible for intelligence to change, check, control or govern functional action. To do so would be to put the effect before the cause. If the brain is operated by the same power which operates the heart, stomach, liver and kidneys, then the functioning of all these organs must be absolutely beyond the reach or control of intelligence, because there can be no intelligence until after they have acted.

But it is a fact to be reckoned with that the mind does control functional action; that in all probability, it consciously or unconsciously controls *all* functional action. In a recent work on "The Force of Mind," Alfred T. Schofield, M. D., M. R. C. S. (I give all the tail to his name to show that he is Orthodox) cites instances where the mind has unmistakably caused paralysis, tumors, the formation of pus, dropsy, fatal hydrophobia, a stricture of the windpipe resulting in death, and in fact, nearly the whole category of functional diseases, and not a few of the cases resulting in actual changes in the organic structure of the body; and he goes further, and shows that the mind which can cause, may also cure all these ailments. If this be true, and it is unquestionably so, then it is not possible that the mind should be the result of these functions over which it has such absolute power.

There is still another mechanical difficulty in the way of the materialistic theory of thought. Every mechanic knows that we can never get quite as much energy out of a machine as we put into it. There is always some loss in friction, internal resistance, etc. Thus, the steam engine gives us only a comparatively small percentage of the potential energy of the coal which is consumed; much of the coal power is lost in various ways before it appears in the engine as actual working energy. The best dynamos give back ninety-five per cent of energy expended in running them; the other five per cent is lost in the transformation from steam power to electrical energy. All any machine can do is to transmute the potential energy of nature into kinetic energy, and no machine can give off as kinetic energy quite all the potential energy which it receives. The human body can be no exception to this law. If it manifests kinetic energy, then it receives potential energy which it transmutes into work power; and if thought is produced in the human body, then we receive some form of potential energy which we transform into thought. There is no escape from this proposition.

This brings us to the ubiquitous stomach. Does thought power come from food? Is there indeed, as Ingersoll said a "wonderful chemistry by which a piece of bread becomes thought"? If so then thought power is supplied to the brain by the stomach. The most plausible supposition would be that it is supplied to the brain in the form of potential energy, and changed into thought in the brain. I suppose no one will assert that it is the stomach which thinks, and supplies the brain with readymade thoughts. If the materialistic psychology is true, the potential energy of food is supplied to the brain by the stomach, just as the potential energy of coal is supplied to the dynamo by the steam engine, and then this energy is changed to thought by the brain, just as steam power is changed to electricity by the dynamo. If this be true, remember that according to the immutable law of mechanics stated above, the brain can only give back a portion - say ninety-five per cent - of the energy which it receives from the stomach. Brain power must always be a little less than stomach power.

Here the mechanical difficulties begin. "We are all conscious that it takes power to run the stomach. Why do we feel dull, heavy, and lethargic after a too-hearty meal? Even the materialist knows that it is because so much power is required for the work of ridding the stomach of its burden that there is none left for thought. But does the brain furnish power to the stomach? If not, how can it be called upon when the stomach is overloaded? If the stomach transmutes bread into thought power, how is it that a little too much bread stops thought? One would think that the reverse would be true, and that the more we ate the better we could think. Materialistic psychology absolutely ignores the fact that it takes power to digest food, and tracing all energy of mind and body to the stomach, is unable to locate or explain the power which operates the stomach itself.

But this is not the worst difficulty. If the stomach is the source of brain power, it must of course be entirely impossible for the brain to control or operate the stomach in any way. The law governing the transmission of power would prevent this. For instance, suppose the dynamo should say to the engine: "Here, hold on! I am going to operate *you* for a while. I will start you when I please, stop you when I please, run you backward or forward, control you in every way." We know this would be impossible, because the dynamo receives its power from the engine, and can only give back ninety-five per cent of what it receives; and so the secondary machine cannot turn, and control the primary one. Broadly speaking, the machine which can start, stop and control the other is the one which is furnishing the power. And no one who is familiar with the phenomena of nutrition will dispute that it is within the power of the brain to start, stop and control the stomach. Thought causes the saliva and the gastric juice to flow; thought can cause vomiting, or absolutely stop digestion; thought can cause the worst forms of dyspepsia.

These, and other facts which the experience of the reader will supply prove that the stomach is the dynamo, and the brain the propelling engine; that there is no chemistry by which bread becomes thought, and that mental action is the cause and not the result of digestion. Without giving further space to the materialistic theory, we will in the next article take up the counter proposition: That mind is an independent entity, not produced by the body.

Mental Storage

In this article I shall draw rather heavily from the ideas advanced in "Brain and Personality," a recent book by William Hanna Thomson, M. D., LL. D. (whom, also, you will perceive by the tail to his name to belong to the ranks of the Very Regular and Exceedingly Orthodox). In spite of his regularity, however, he has written a really scientific book, and the substance of his contention is that the mind is not produced by the brain, but that the mind shapes the brain for its own purposes; that thought really makes the brain, instead of the brain making thought. He calls the brain the "physical organ of the mind."

It is a fact pretty well known to most people that the exercise of certain powers and faculties is dependent upon certain localities in the brain. That mental faculties and powers correspond with the development of certain parts of the brain has long been a belief, the so-called science of phrenology was founded upon this idea, which is not without a foundation in fact. It is not true, as we shall show further on, that the shape of the skull, or the development of certain brain areas fix irrevocably the character, powers and destiny of the individual. It is a fact, however, that all mental functions are absolutely dependent upon the physical integrity of certain definite and particular areas of the brain. There is, for instance, a brain center for speech; and an injury to this area will render the person incapable of speaking, even though he can read and understand spoken words as well as ever. And, separate and distinct from this speech center, there is a brain locality with which reading is done, and an injury to this place will cause a person to forget how to read, while he will retain his ability to speak perfectly.

Your brain is like a phonograph record, upon which you store up the things you want to bring out afterward. You learn speech long before you learn to read, and have a brain place stored with the sound of spoken words; then when you learn to read, you engrave upon another brain place the appearance of printed and written words; the mind takes these things and writes them upon the brain, and an injury to any brain locality destroys the record written there, and paralyzes some power or faculty which was dependent upon that record for its existence. This injury might be from the bursting of a minute artery, which is a thing you can cause by overeating, and which is the most common cause of paralysis. Mr. Thomson cites many cases, among them that of a lady who lost the power to read, while retaining speech and hearing perfectly, and of a "gentleman who one morning lost not only all power of utterance, but also all ability to read. He could, however, hear words perfectly, and strange to tell, he proved that the place for arithmetical figures is in a different brain locality from that for words, because he could read and write figures and calculate every kind of sum in large business transactions, which he successfully conducted for seven years afterward, without once being able to speak a word or even to read his own signature." It appears that music notes are registered in a still different place, for several instances are on record of musicians who have lost all power to read music, while retaining their ability to read everything else, and of others who have become "word blind" as it is called, while still able to read music. When a person becomes a musician, he simply engraves certain knowledge upon a certain locality in his brain. Note this, for I shall refer to it again.

And each different language that we learn has a different

locality. Mr. Thomson cites the case of an Englishman who could speak French, Latin and Greek. He became word blind in English, could read French only imperfectly, Latin a little better, and Greek as well as ever, "showing that his English record was ruined, his French record damaged, his Latin one less so, while his Greek record had escaped entirely." Does not all this go to prove that the brain is only a recording or transmitting instrument for the personality behind it?

What I am trying to do is to pile up convincing evidence that the brain is not the source of thought, but is merely the instrument of the one who thinks, just as the piano is the instrument of the one who plays, and when I am sure that I have done this, to find what practical conclusions we may draw from this basic fact. It is now a well-established fact that we only use one-half of the brain in thinking, and that the other half is not concerned in thought or knowledge. In a vast majority of people - that is, in all right-handed persons - the thinking is all done with the left half of the brain; and all the knowledge is inscribed upon that hemisphere. An injury to the right half of the brain will cause paralysis of some muscle on the left side, but it will not cause loss of memory, word blindness, or any of the mental phenomena referred to above. The left side of the brain we use for thought, for the retention of knowledge, and also to control the motions of the right side of the body; the right side of the brain is used to control the movements of the left side of the body, but not in thought or knowledge. With left-handed people the case is reversed.

Now, the inference we draw from this is that we are born with two blank records. No newborn child knows how to speak, or write, or think. He will not be able to speak until he makes a speaking place in his brain; he will not be able to write until he makes a writing place in his brain; and he immediately sets to work to make a brain through which he can express himself. And, as both halves of the brain are equally available for the purpose, he naturally uses that one with which he begins to make gestures, etc., to express his desires. The beginning of language is gesture, and it is natural that the speech center should be developed in that hemisphere of the brain first used as intelligence begins to express itself in motion.

That is why the thought centers are in the left brain of a right-handed person, and *vice versa*.

Up to a certain age the brain remains plastic enough so that if an injury occurs to the thought brain, the person can begin over again and create new knowledge centers in the other hemisphere. This has happened in many cases where young people have lost certain powers or faculties by cerebral lesions, and have afterward recovered these faculties by developing new centers in the other brain. It rarely happens after the age of forty-five, and the reason is because most persons after passing that age soon clog their brains with calcareous matter by overeating, and destroy the plasticity of their brains by filling them with food waste. If all people past the age of forty-five would live on twelve ounces or less of solid food per day, we should soon find that one may receive new ideas as readily at seventy-five as at fifteen. You cannot do it, however, if your brain is a hardened mass of waste matter. If you overeat, you will be "sot" in your ways, and a has-been at fifty. Keep your phonograph records soft and receptive.

All this throws new light upon the problem of the child. Here he lies in his cradle, with no impression as yet made upon either hemisphere of his brain; shall he be a musician, an orator, a poet, a philanthropist, a mechanic or a murderer? It all depends upon what the mysterious personality concealed within that organism shall write upon that brain. In which direction will it start? There are certain tendencies there, inherited from his ancestry, which will pull him strongly in certain directions, but we rejoice to know that there is not a single hereditary tendency which cannot be overcome by writing opposing facts upon the brain. It is not a question of "training" the child, or of "developing his mind"; the real question is whether or not we can get him to perform the labor of building the right kind of a brain. If he builds a music center there, he will be a musician; if he builds a language center he will he an orator; what he writes upon that record he will be able to express, and nothing else. And while it is no doubt true that the child will find it easier to inscribe some things upon his brain than it is to inscribe certain others, it is also a fact that no child born with a normal brain is incapable of learning anything in art, music, oratory or mechanics - all things are possible to them that believe. The blank brain leaves are there, waiting for the inscription; the child may write upon them what he will. And it is all a matter of will with him, as it is with you and me.

Curing Bad Habits

The problem of the child is not whether we can save him, or whether God can save him, but whether we can induce him to save himself. For in this matter of brain building there is no vicarious atonement, no salvation by proxy. Just as no one person can learn to swim for another; so it is true that no one person can learn any lesson for another. Every inscription that is placed upon the brain tablets must be engraved there by our own effort, and often that effort must be patient, persistent and long continued.

Think of the persistent and long-continued effort by which a child learns to talk; it is only be repetitions running sometimes into years that some words are at last properly registered upon the record of the brain. Many, many, sometimes almost countless repetitions are necessary to the writing of some records; others are easier to get. If it were not for his desires the child would never learn to talk; he wants things, and he tries to ask for them; he wants to know things, and he tries to ask questions, and in these repeated efforts word after word is written in the word place of his brain. When the older person learns a new language the process is exactly the same; by persistent effort, word after word is written in its place in the brain until they are all there.

There are some people who say that they cannot learn languages; they mean that the task is so unattractive to them that they do not put forth the necessary effort of will to concentrate the mind, and do the required work. So of those who say they "cannot learn music"; they mean that their desire to learn is not strong enough to cause the necessary concentration of mind, and to continue it until the required knowledge is written in the brain place for music. Any person of normal brain can learn anything that is to be learned, or become anything that is possible to any other person; it is all a matter of will. The hereditary traits which burden us most are those of desire. If you do not want to be something, you will hardly try hard and long enough to be anything. But just as it is certain that you can write what you will upon a slate, so is it certain that you can write what you will upon your brain; and what you write there you will be.

There is often, however, no labor requiring more concentrated effort and more severe self-discipline than brain building. For this reason, most people are, in many things like a man who starts in to learn some foreign tongue, and after acquiring such a smattering of it as to be able to express himself very poorly indeed, gives up the struggle, and goes on through life without ever being able to make himself really understood. Too many brain records are fragmentary and incomplete for lack of the necessary labor to make them perfect.

Remember that the brain is the instrument through which the real personality expresses himself, and he can only express what is already written there. Consequently, the external man will be just what is inscribed upon his brain, for all his actions must be dictated or directed through these brain records. You cannot saw wood with a hammer; nor can the soul play a piano with the fingers until the knowledge of piano playing is written in the music place of the brain. You cannot show forth a high and noble personality until you have written within your skull a record of noble and holy desires; according to the tools you give it, so will the expression of your soul be. You can wind up a phonograph, and you may make it run fast or slow, but you cannot make it say anything that is not on the records. If some one had put his opinion of you on a record, even though you knew that opinion to be untrue, you could not make the record tell the truth; the only thing possible would be to make another.

You have written your opinion of yourself upon your brain; you cannot be anything else until you change the record. It is not necessary to destroy the old record, or to obliterate it. Suppose a man learns English and German; he has them both written, each in its own place in his brain; he did not have to rub out the English in order to learn German; and though he was born an Englishman, and learned the English language in his babyhood, if he persistently continues to use the German speech instead of his mother tongue he will come in time to be more fluent in German than in English; and in time he will prefer to use the German, and will *think* in that tongue, because it is easiest for him. So, if you have a habit or a trait written on your brain, and do not want to use *that* record any more, what you will have to do is to build another, and better record to use in place of it. There is no other way.

Now, this is very important, for if it be true, all things are possible unto us; we can develop any power or faculty we desire to develop, we can be anything we choose to be, we can form any habit we desire to form. Understand what I mean by forming habits; I hold that there is no such thing as quitting a habit; the thing to do is to form a counter-habit. As I have said, if you have a bad habit of mind or body, you need not try to destroy the brain-place upon which the thought that causes it is written; write the opposite thought upon another brain-place, and ever after express yourself through *that*. Suppose you have written this opinion of yourself: That you are little, and feeble, and stooped, and hollow-chested, and afraid of your shadow, and are going to die soon; well, if you do not want that to be true, you will have to write upon another place that you are big, and upstanding and straight, and brave, and can live as long as you want to; and when you get it written, express yourself through that place, instead of through the old one. In time, it will be easiest to use the new place, and the old one will be so rusty that you cannot use it if you would.

This enables us to state the philosophy of being and of attainment with scientific accuracy, and to describe the process minutely. I want to give some specific instructions, and I want to close this article by proving to those who have passed middle life that as much may be accomplished by them as by the young; that no matter who you are, you're not too old. I said in a former article that the reason why old people do not learn easily, lose their memories, etc., is that they eat more food than is required for the maintenance of the body, and the waste clogs the brain. You remember that Metchnikoff, not long ago, told the world that old age was really caused by the presence of an acrid poison in the intestines, causing the white blood-corpuscles to refuse to perform their functions; and heralded to the world with a great flourish of trumpets the alleged fact that sour milk would neutralize the poison, and that faithful swill drinking would give us bodily immortality.

The swill cure seems to have gone to join goat-lymph, and Brown-Sequard's elixir of life. If Metchnikoff had not been "regular" he would have known that the acrid poison in the intestines is the direct result of eating more food than the system could assimilate; and he would have simply said, "Eat less, and you will stay young."

Cornaro, the wise Italian, tried the truly scientific plan. A broken-down wreck at forty-five, he reduced his allowance of solid food to twelve ounces per day and died at one hundred, retaining his mental vigor to the last. And he noticed that whenever, at the solicitation of his physicians, he increased his allowance he "began to grow irritable" and to lose his mental powers. After a hearty meal you begin to lose *your* mental powers, for the same reason that it is hard for an old dog to learn new tricks. The old dog lies - or sits - around, and eats until his brain cells are clogged with waste food matter; let him take a good long fast, and you will be surprised to see him develop a puppyish aptitude for learning now tricks. Try it yourself; fast until your mind is clear, and then eat little and with care, and when you find yourself "growing irritable" or losing your mental poise, cut down the food supply. You are not too old to learn; you are too well fed to learn, and that is all.

Desire and Self-Culture

Whether you are young or old, let us now suppose that your brain is plastic enough to receive new impressions, and that there is some definite thing in the way of self-culture that you wish to accomplish. Fix clearly in your mind, first, that it is going to be wholly a matter of *will* whether you succeed or not, and be sure you fully understand the difference between willing to do, and wanting to do. One man may glance at the heading of this article and say, "I want to read that" and pass on without reading it; another sees it, and says, "I *will* read that" and he reads it. "I want to" does not mold the brain; "I will" does. If you ever get to be what you want to be, you will have to will to be what you want to be.

Let us suppose, again, that what you wish to attain is something in the line of health. You, the soul, the mind, the real personality, wish to build a perfectly healthy body, and you can only do it through the brain, for that is your medium of communication with the body. There are records in the brain which compel you to express ill health, just as a crooked ruler compels you to make a crooked mark; you will have to quit expressing yourself through these records, and make another, which shall express health; not the desire of health, but the assertion of health. Understand - it will do no good to write upon your brain the thought that you want to be well. You have not written there now the thought that you want to be sick, but the thought that you *are* sick and that thought is finding expression in your body; write now the thought that you *are* well, and that thought will find physical expression.

And you do not have to imagine anything to be true which is not true, or to make any false assertions; you, the intelligence, the mind, are really well; you are making a crooked mark because you are using a crooked stick. You can turn the crank, all right, but the phonograph will only say the words that are on the record. You will have to make a record which has on it the words you want the machine to say. Now, it is absolutely certain that you can do this, but it is pretty sure to take some time, and a considerable effort of will. Instances are by no means rare where a brain record has been created in a flash, and an instantaneous cure effected; but in the great majority of cases it is like learning a new language, or like a child learning his first one - a work requiring wearisome effort and repetition. And whether the task is easy or hard depends mostly on desire. It is easier to use the will in concentration or assertion, when desire is strong.

And that is where heredity gets in its work on you. Desire is hereditary, but capability is not. One man, by heredity, may have a liking for a particular food; but all men, by nature, have the power to masticate and swallow that food. You may say of yourself, "I cannot learn to play the piano; I have no musical talent," You have as much musical talent as any one ever had, but your desire is not strong enough to induce you to put forth the effort necessary to train your muscles; or rather, to create a brain place for each muscular movement. Oh, I know! You say you want to play the piano as badly as any one ever did; and I admit it. You want to produce sweet and harmonious sounds, but you do *not* want mechanical excellence badly enough to concentrate your mind on your fingers; and you will have to make a brain place for each finger movement before you can play, and use that brain place until its control of the muscles is habitual and automatic. You sit at the piano desiring music, but not finger skill; that is why you have no "musical talent." You do not learn music because there is a "kink" in your desire, and you do not control your attention. It takes will and attention to mold a brain.

Let me make this plain by another illustration. People say to me: "I have no memory for names. If I am introduced to a person, I can remember his face very well, but if I meet him on the street the next day, I invariably find that I have forgotten his name." You never heard his name. You could not have told it two minutes after you were introduced to him. You looked at his face, and thought of his face, and gave all your attention to his face, none to his name. You remember the things you give attention to; you learn the things you give attention to, provided that attention is constant and concentrated enough to make the necessary brain impression. And, given a brain in a normal condition of plasticity, if there is anything which any one else has learned, or can learn, it is an absolute certainty that you can learn that thing if you can give your attention to it. And if there is anything that anybody else has been, or can be, it is absolutely certain that you can be that thing if yon can give your attention to it for a sufficient time.

We shall soon be able to make self-culture a process of mathematical exactness. If you wish to learn a thing, we know exactly what you have to do. You must give your attention to it until it is inscribed upon its own brain place. If you wish to learn to do a thing, you must give your attention to it until the method of doing it is written on its own brain place, and until the necessary muscles are brought under control. If you wish to be a thing, you must write upon the proper brain place the assertion that you *are* that thing, and then express yourself through that brain place.

You will see how logical and natural all this makes the New Thought propositions. It gives us a physical basis for reasoning to the metaphysical; it proves that mind forms brain, and that brain cannot produce mind. It proves that Personality is greater than brain, and can give expression through brain, to whatsoever it will; it proves that Personality is sufficiently independent of brain to be able to mold and fashion brain as a potter fashions clay; and gives us ground for the inference that Personality may exist apart from brain, and after brain is no more. And it is all perfectly logical, reaching its conclusions by reasoning from effect to cause, and without a flaw in its deductions, or its manner of making them.

It gives us a physical ground for faith in the soul's power of accomplishment. And this is a great thing; for without faith there can be no real effort; no concentration, no controlling of the attention. The will is never really exerted without faith. When, therefore, we have explained in detail the physical mechanism through which mind expresses itself; and when we have described the process of attainment in such simple words that he who runs may read and understand; when we have given a mathematical demonstration of the fact that it is possible for each to do and be all that any may do and be - have we not made faith easy, and contributed something of value to the world's life? I think we have.

Road to Power

Wallace D. Wattles

Two Kinds of People

There are two kinds of people in the world, those who count and those who do not. The vast majority are of those who do not count. They are born; they grow to maturity; they eat, drink, sleep and work; they marry and are given in marriage; they laugh and are happy, and they are sick and miserable in turn; they die, and except as they leave behind them children to do as they have done it is as if they had never lived at all. They are the children of circumstance, the creatures of environment. Their lives are ordered for them by custom and habit; they think the thoughts and imitate the actions of those with whom they chance to be associated. They exercise no power beyond that which is common to their fellows; they leave no footprints on the sands of time. When the census is taken they are counted; but in so far as a really distinct individuality is concerned they do not count. It would answer as well to take their census in blocks of ten as one by one; or to reckon them by the hundred like sheep, for sheep have almost as much individuality as they. They may be more or less happy, more or less useful, more or less successful; but even though they gain wealth they do not count, for their riches do not give them a distinct personality.

Over against these are the few who lead the Powerful Life. These are the real movers of things; they are known and felt. It is not that they are superior to the others in education or talent, for they are not; some of the most powerful people in the world show little of talent or genius and have none of what the world calls education, while some of the "educated" are ineffective. The power which makes people count is neither physical or mental; it is not conditional on strength of body or of mind. It is not a special gift; the effective ones are not so because they use a power which is denied to others, but because they use a power which others have but do not use.

One man says something and says it well but the world goes on unheeding. Another man says the same thing, perhaps with blundering tongue and uncouth words, and all men pause and hear with bated breath, for he speaks with power. One man writes a book of truth, faultless in style and diction; the world reads and lays it calmly down, saying only that it is very good. Another man writes the same things with far less of scholarship; and the book is a living thing, on all men's tongues, for every reader feels the touch of power.

Two men take up their abode in a community; one is a man of education and ability and his advent is heralded with a flourish of trumpets; he comes well advertised. But he is soon lost to view in the common life; he becomes merely one among others. With all his gifts he does not make his individuality felt; he does not exercise power. The other comes, perhaps poor and unknown, possessing little of education or training; but in a few months his name is known to every man, woman and child, and there is talk of running him for Public office. He has this subtle, indefinable, almost incomprehensible something which I am trying to describe; his word is with power.

Power is not conditioned upon special mental or spiritual gifts, nor upon righteousness. One of the most powerful men I ever met was a gambler and a most unscrupulous political boss; a man whose name, synonymous with dirty politics, was execrated in half a dozen states. He was not of course, without his good traits; but they were greatly overshadowed by his evil ones. Yet he had power. There was power in the keen glance of his eye and in the low tone of his voice; power in the firm grasp of his hand, and power radiated from his whole personality. Many a time I have felt him come silently into a room where a score of people were gathered, and turning my head to look have found him there. You did not have to see or hear him to know when he was near; he could be felt.

The career of Napoleon illustrates again the fact that power is not conditioned on righteousness. Consider how marvelous his performance was. A poor young Corsican lieutenant, then general of armies, emperor of France and master of Europe, making and unmaking kings. Yet it seems that he was coldly selfish and often very cruel, and he scrupled at nothing in order to accomplish his purpose. But his word was with power.

There are good men also, who exercise power. Take the case of Dwight L. Moody, a man of no imposing presence and of little oratorical ability. He only talked to his great audiences in a common, straightforward fashion, and yet multitudes were swayed by his personality and thousands were converted. His word, also, was with power. There went a power out from him which reached the hearts of men. The power was not in the words but in the man - or behind the man. I have heard of another evangelist at whose look people sometimes burst into tears although they did not know who or what he was. It was power.

The story of Samson, in the book of Judges, is an excellent illustration of the thing I am trying to make plain. The power of Samson was not in his muscles, for when his hair was shorn it departed from him; and yet it was not in his hair. It was in that which the unshorn locks symbolized the state of being a Nazarite unto God. It was something greater than the possible strength of mere flesh and bone. When he grasped the gate of the walled city it was torn from its fastenings as though it had been but a puny affair of sticks or straws. No muscles did that; muscles could not do it. It was power.

If you do not believe the Samson story, go look at a great electro-magnet. You will see a large crooked iron bar wound with copper wire, inert and powerless; but close the circuit and send the current through the coils, and the magnet will lift a ton of iron; a thing on the face of it quite impossible for it to do. It is unthinkable that a piece of iron should exert such tremendous force; we would not believe it if we did not see it. It is no more marvelous that a man should tear the gates of a city from the wall or pull the great beam from the loom, when his hair had been woven into the web, than for an electro magnet to lift a ton.

Let us consider for the purpose of illustration that the Samson story is literally true; and that power was applied through him in some such way as it is applied through the electro magnet. But Samson used the power intelligently; He directed it and moved what he pleased while what he did not please to move he let alone. It was the same power that is in the magnet, as I am going to show you later on; there is only one power.

The political boss used it for the accomplishment of his vicious purposes; Napoleon used it to gain the ends of his selfish ambition and Moody used it to bring souls to God. But it is all one power and it is at the service of any man who will lay hold upon it and use it; it is at his service for the saving of souls, the healing of his own body or the bodies of others, the doing of deeds of love, and not the less for gaining his personal selfish aims and objects. But it is certain to bring him to disaster in the end as it did Samson, Napoleon and the other I have mentioned, unless he shall use it nobly; and for this there is good reason, as we shall see when we proceed a little farther with our study. It is possible for any man or woman to exercise power; to develop personality, and to become effective; and it is well for all to remember that while the right use of power can only result in peace and happiness, those who misuse it are subject to terrible penalties. Of that we shall speak again.

Whence Comes the Power?

That there is a powerful life; that it may be lived here; that it may be lived by any one, we are obliged to concede; and having conceded this we cannot fail to wish to live this life for rightly lived, it means health, wealth, power and happiness. Those who read this series of lessons are going to learn how to live it, and they need first to understand a little as to what the power is and whence it comes. We are just passing from the physical, animal or material stage of development to the mental and spiritual stage. We are ceasing to be physical men and women and becoming mental and spiritual men and women. To make this change is sometimes a matter of considerable difficulty. The great majority of people are not as yet making it at all. They are still entirely material in their beliefs and thought. They do not see the world of Spirit; they put their faith in houses and lands and money and so on, and because they believe in those things they are subject to them. The only powerful life of which they conceive is a life of physical power.

New Thought people, they whose spiritual eyes are becoming opened; who begin to see the inner and finer penetrating the false appearances of the world of matter; who begin to see Spirit as the cause of matter and of what are called natural phenomena; these are they who begin to see the Kingdom of God. They get glimpses of a powerful life which may be lived in the flesh and here on earth; occasionally they enter upon it and live it for a time, but their great difficulty is lack of understanding as to what the power is and how the life must be lived. This we are going to find out.

The first step is to learn the great truth about the universe which is that all is one. All things are forms of one Substance; that Substance is conscious and intelligent; it is Spirit. In former articles and in my books I have referred to this Original Substance under various names, as the supreme, the Thinking Stuff, God, All-Mind and so on; but throughout these lessons I shall use the one word, Spirit. Substance is Spirit; everything is Spirit; there isn't anything but Spirit. Before you can fully believe this great truth you will have to learn to disbelieve much that your senses tell you, and it is easy to do this when you understand how unreliable the senses are. The physical man depends upon the senses for everything. To him seeing is believing, and accepts as real the appearance around him; but in reality he is grossly deceived; he lives in an unreal world, his whole universe is a deception, and not what it seems to him at all.

This man must believe that he lives on a flat world under a solid blue arch; the sun and moon travel over him and his earth is stationary and the stars are small points of light. There are appearances of the physical world as given us by the senses, yet no civilized person now really believes in them; we know that the earth is round, that the sky is not solid, that the stars are very much larger than the earth, and that the earth goes round the sun. No well-informed person believes what he sees as to these things; he looks through appearances to the reality.

Take another illustration. Nothing appears more real than color and one can hardly doubt that the objects around us are really of the hue they appear; that the grass is green and the robin's breast is red and so on. But there is no color except in consciousness. When an object appeal's to us to be of a given color, as red, it is not really so. The "red" object reflects or refuses to absorb and receive the red in the ray of light which strikes it and throws it back to the eye; we see the color it rejects and not the color it is. Where there is no eye to receive the reflection color has no existence. So it does not do to believe appearances to be true; we must look through them and see the only reality, and the only reality of all things is Spirit. The first step to be taken by those who would lead the Powerful Life is to cease to be misled by appearances, and to perceive truth. To cease to believe in what seems to be, and to have faith in what is. They must get to the heart of things, and instead of trying to reason from appearances to realities they must believe realities and disregard appearances.

Spirit is Substance and all Substance is Spirit. There cannot be two Substances. The moment we admit that there are two Substances as Spirit and matter we are absolutely lost. If matter is something distinct from Spirit then it has powers and potentialities of its own and may affect us for good or ill. So, if we believe this, we shall become more and more tied down to matter which we can see and have less and less faith in Spirit which we cannot see or can only feel; and the Powerful Life will become impossible to us. We must see that Spirit is Substance and that it is the only Substance. Nothing exists but Spirit.

Next we must come to understand that Spirit is life, and that it is all the life there is. Nothing lives but Spirit. Every thought of man, every volition of any animal, every unfoldment of leaf or blossom is Spirit, acting in the thing that moves. Spirit lives in the grass and flowers and trees; in flesh and insect; in animals and men. There is no life but the life of Spirit. Nothing has individual life or life of its own. It is all the life of Spirit.

Again, all power is spirit. Every movement in nature or art from the flutter of a leaf to the rushing of the giant current through the dynamo formed by man is Spirit. And in it all and through it all Spirit is working intelligently to some great purpose or purposes of His own. That there is intelligence through the power of nature is shown for one thing among many by continuity. Everything works under the same laws, yesterday, today and forever. But suppose one day the water pipes ran water and the next day gasoline; one day you weighed one hundred and ten pounds and the next day half a ton, the laws of gravity and chemistry working in contrary fashion; then you might suspect that there were two forces in nature or that the one force was an unintelligent one.

If you want to live the Powerful Life of Samson, Napoleon, or of the evangelist - and you do, you are reaching out for more power. That is what we are all seeking. Whether we want merely to become rich or whether we wish to excel in society or to rear our children well or to become benefactors of humanity, the only thing we require is power and ability to lead the Powerful Life. At the close of this second chapter I bring you to this fact, which if you grasp it fully, will give you the foundation on which you must stand in leading the life, and if you go on with the succeeding lessons will certainly enable you to lead it.

We live and move and have our being in the limitless ocean of intelligent Spirit from whom we draw our life and power, physical, mental and spiritual. All power is in this Spirit. And we may learn to so unify ourselves with Spirit that more and more power shall be ours, in fact we may have all the power that He can trust us with, and it is only then, a matter of making ourselves trustworthy.

The Road to Power

I do not pretend to say that all who have lived the Powerful Life have accepted the proposition laid down at the close of the last chapter. Most of them never heard such a statement formulated. I do say, however, that you cannot live the life consciously, purposefully and intelligently unless you accept those propositions, and unless you have some degree of comprehension as to what they mean. To get this comprehension you will have to THINK, and if you are one of those who are too far gone in the prevailing habit of intellectual laziness to think, you may as well stop here. There is no labor so severe and trying as sustained and consecutive thinking; and there is no labor from which the average person, whether male or female, shrinks as from the work of thought.

I have in mind a woman who was trying to demonstrate health by New Thought and who complained of her ill success, but when she was cited to a series of articles then running in a certain magazine which applied to her case, she said: "I saw those, but the title sounded so dry that I did not read them." She wanted something lively and interesting to read; something she could read without being compelled to think. She was trying to cure herself by thought, but without thinking.

She was one of a large number of people who spend their lives running away from thought. Their passion for mental forgetfulness fills the moving picture shows and crowds the cheap amusement houses. Their leisure time is spent hunting for an emotional chloroform which shall make thought impossible; and the result is that they stay right where they are, neither advancing or losing ground, but going around in a circle, year after year, and always arriving at the place from which they started. It is the penalty they pay for refusing to think. Nothing can accomplish the emancipation of the race but thought. If you are to lead the Powerful Life you must not shrink from thought.

You must put yourself into the right relationship with the Supreme Intelligence; you must learn to see what God is doing and get into the vibration that now thrills the universe. There is nothing but Spirit; nothing moves or has the least power, or acts in any way whatsoever, but Spirit. Nothing is conscious but Spirit; Spirit is all, and Spirit is one. There is not One Great Spirit who rules over a host of lesser spirits. If there are lesser spirits having life, power and consciousness, then God is neither all-powerful or omniscient; and the universe is not a harmonious whole, but the playground or the battleground, as the case may be, of different forces and intelligences. Just as the blades of grass are not separate lives, but one life vitalizing many organisms, so men are not separate and intelligent spirits, but one Spirit expressing Himself consciously in different forms as He expresses life in the different blades of grass. Man is not a soul or a spirit; he is Spirit.

Man is Spirit. He has no soul, spirit or ego; there is no human ego; there is only Spirit. Spirit knows all that is known and performs every act mental or physical. Man has no mind; he is Mind. Man has no ego, he does not think; Spirit thinks. To say that man thinks is to admit that there is something which acts which is not Spirit, and our whole structure falls in ruins. If a man has life in himself, power in himself, and thinks in himself, then he will concern himself very little about God; and as man appears to himself to be a separate entity, most men do give themselves very little concern about God. But the man of the senses, like the rainbow or the color on the robin's breast, is only an appearance; he is the reflection of the reality, and the reality is Spirit. Man's senses give him consciousness of himself as a form, and make him conscious of the fact that he is surrounded by other forms; and he believes those forms to be separate realities. But there is only one reality and that is Spirit.

Consciousness unformed is unlimited; there can be no limit to that which has no form, for if there is no form there are no boundaries. The consciousness of unformed Spirit is unlimited but the consciousness of Spirit in any form is limited by the perceptive powers of the form. Man's consciousness is limited by the range of his perceptive powers, and he can only increase his perceptive powers by thought. And yet man's thoughts are the cause of all his errors and departures from truth. If he makes the effort of separate thinking he is sure to fall into more or less of error and perhaps into much suffering. But his suffering will bring him to the real truth, broaden his perception, and so increase his power.

The Powerful Life is that condition in which the power of

Spirit plays through the channels of man's thought as power flowed through Samson; and before this can happen the channels of man's thought must be cleared and consecrated by man's own effort. Samson was a Nazarite, set apart to the service of Spirit; his power was conditional on his retaining his consecration.

Man consecrates himself by trying to find truth. Just in proportion as we really want truth, and want to do right, do we advance toward unity with Spirit. It is not enough to want more life or enjoyment; the essential thing is to want to be right. When we earnestly desire to do the right thing we begin to think our way towards the truth that underlies appearances; and that truth is Spirit.

Spirit knows everything; all that has been, all that is, and all that will be, are present to the consciousness of that Infinite Mind in which you live, and move, and are. Every truth is present in God's mind as a thought; and when you perceive a truth you perceive a thought of God. The man who can perceive the thoughts of God, and who has the Will to Do Right has entered upon the Powerful Life.

To will to do right is to will to do the will of God; and the will of God is that all should have more abundant life. If it is your will to give more life to every living thing in so far as it lies in your power to do so, then you will do right. But it must be an active will and intention, not a mere benevolent willingness or desire. To wish all men well is good as far as it goes, but it is not enough; the Will to Do Right requires the active DETERMINATION AND INTENTION to give more life to every person, whenever we have the opportunity. The Will to Do Right puts you in harmony with God, and brings your mind into close touch with His Mind that you may perceive His thoughts; and the perception of truth will begin to come to you. To have the Will to Do Right; to know the Right Thing to Do and to have the Power to Do the Right Thing; he who has these essentials can do what he wants to do and become what he wants to become.

Your Invisible Power

Wallace D. Wattles

What is Truth?

Time

The science of theology and medicine are necessarily very closely allied, both having to do with the saving of men from the consequences of wrong living; and it follows that in religion and medicine we are always seeking for realities; searching the truth; seeking the ultimate, spiritual and physical facts upon which to base our theories, and from which to proceed in making our demonstrations of health and wholeness. And since our demonstrations must and will be complete or incomplete just in proportion to the completeness of our grasp of the realities, the importance of the search for truth becomes apparent; the very first thing we have to do is to penetrate through all the appearances of life, and ascertain the differences between what is really true and what is only apparently true; for there is often a vast difference between the appearance and the reality.

The sun appears to rise and set, and to go around the earth; but it does not. A balloon goes up; and a stone falls to the earth; in appearance there are two forces at work, but in reality there is only one: gravity. The reality behind the going up of the balloon and the coming down of the stone is the same. And to seek for the realities behind the appearances of life, behind its goings up and comings down, its goings out and comings in - that is science, and that is what we are going to try to do.

The first of the realities with which we will deal is Time. It is the fashion with some metaphysical writers to assert that there is no time; but the arguments advanced in support of this claim are superficial. Time is not an entity having substance, but it is an existing reality, nevertheless. Time is not an idea; a fiction by which we measure and record the motions of the heavenly bodies; time would go on just the same and at exactly the same rate if the heavenly bodies were motionless. Do not misunderstand me in my use of the word "time." Many people suppose that time began when man began, and must end when man ends as a mortal and physical being, and that the periods before and after the earth life of the human race are to be called eternities;

in other words that there can be no time except so long as there is a mortal man to measure it; but this is erroneous.

Days, weeks, months and years must have gone on before man came on earth, just as they do now; and if man disappeared from the earth, they would still go on. If the earth ceased to revolve around the sun, and to turn on its axis, the succession of the seasons and of day and night would cease; day would be continuous on one side of the earth, and night upon the other, but hours and minutes would go on just the same, and if the sun, moon, planets, stars and all else were to disappear and be succeeded by black, silent, formless chaos, hours and minutes would go on forever. Clocks do not make time; an hour would have the same duration if there were no clocks. In eternity there must still be time; time is duration in eternity. Eternity is endless time.

Time can never end. If you try to think of a point at which time should end, you can only think of it as a point beyond which there must be still more time. Also, then, time can never have had a beginning; for if you try to think of a point at which time began, you can only think of it as a point beyond which there must have been still more time. Do not say that endless time is unthinkable; you can very easily think endless time, if you do not try to think of the end of it. You cannot *comprehend* endless time, for that means to contain it in your mind, or to go around it; but you can know what it is, and you can know that it is.

Time is; and we must use it, whether we will or not. And the use we make of present time decides the use we shall be able to make of future time; just as the use we made of past time has fixed our place in present time. The use we make of today decides the use we shall be able to make of tomorrow. To be strong and wise is to be able to use time well; and to use time well is to become continually stronger and wiser. Success, growth and development are only attained by the right use of time; and we are failures today in exact proportion as we have erred in our use of time past. To know the right use of the present moment is therefore of immense importance; and to have the will to make the right use of it is more important still. If man can - and will - make the right use of every moment of time, he must certainly become a being of marvelous power and wholeness. Oh, the wasted time! The misspent time! The lost time!

We close this chapter, then, by claiming the demonstration of our first fact; that time is a reality.

-

Space

Bear in mind that in the first chapter we prove that time is an existent reality; in this chapter we shall try to prove that space also exists. Space is the place where a thing is; and it is also the place where no thing is. Space is the place where the earth is; the earth's diameter being about 7,925 miles, it fills so much space; if the earth were to disappear, the 7,925 miles of space would still exist, but it would then be empty space whereas now it is filled space. The sun also, fills space, and the distance between the earth and the sun is space; beyond the sun is more space, and beyond the earth still more; and so on. It does not matter whether space is occupied or unoccupied; empty or filled; it is space, all the same. Space is a reality. Distance is a portion of space between two given points. Endless distance would comprise all of space in one direction.

Space has three dimensions: Length, breadth and thickness. It could never have a beginning, and can never have an ending. If all created things, and all substance should disappear, space would still exist; it would be merely blank, empty space, where now is filled space. Also, space can have no boundaries. If you try to think of a boundary to space, what will you think of as lying beyond the boundary? Something solid? Then that something solid must itself occupy space, while if there is nothing there, that nothing must be unfilled space. So, beyond any boundary that you can set for space, there must be still more space. Space is a reality; beginningless, endless, boundless. Time is a reality; and yet, neither time nor space are substantial things. They possess no power. They do not act, neither can they be acted upon. Time can be used, and space can be occupied; and that is what we do with them; we occupy space and make use of time.

Space is the field in which we must operate, and contains the raw materials which we must use. The claim has been made that space is non-existent to mind or spirit, because it does not require appreciable time for the transference of thought; but the validity of this deduction has not been proved. The distances with which we are able to deal are very limited; it might require a measurable time to send thought to the sun, or to the planet Mars, or for a spirit to travel those distances. Again, the argument is advanced that the moon "acts" on the earth; and that, as a thing cannot act where it is not, there is no space between the moon and the earth; but this is puerile. The moon does not, and cannot act on the earth, because it does not touch the earth; if it affects the earth at all, it must act on something which is between them, and which in turn acts on the earth. And this something which is between the earth and the moon occupies space.

I have spoken of filled space and empty space. I do not know whether empty space exists or not, but it is quite thinkable that, it should exist. There may be portions of empty space, surrounded by filled space; or there may be endless extensions of empty space, side by side with endless extensions of filled space; I do not know. I know that there is filled space, and that there may be empty space. But, if there is filled space, what fills it? The answer to this must be in one word - Substance. That which is not substance is not anything, and that, which is not anything cannot fill space. Space is filled by substance, and cannot be filled by anything else; but what is substance, and how do we know that it exists? That we leave for the next chapter, closing this with the claim that we have demonstrated that we live in space, and that life consists in making use of time.

-

Substance

Substance is that which occupies space. In its more compact and rigid forms substance is perceptible by the senses, and is then called matter; but in its finer and more ethereal forms, when it cannot be perceived by the senses, substance is still matter, and is essentially the same. The apparently many substances of nature are in reality only varying forms of one Substance; the differences between them are due to varying degrees of pressure, and to the form and rate of vibration of the atoms which compose them. Ice is a solid substance; water a partially fluid substance; the vapor arising from water verges on the gaseous state; and oxygen and hydrogen are gases. But a piece of ice may be brought back through all these stages, and converted into oxygen and hydrogen, and no change is made in it except that in the fluid state the atoms are less firmly pressed together than in the solid state; and in the gaseous state the bond of cohesion is still weaker, and the atoms circulate or roll around each other more freely than in the fluid state.

It is now a well-known fact that nearly all the growth of

the vegetable kingdom comes from the atmosphere; trees, plants and flowers are solidified air. The furniture in our homes, and the walls of the houses in which we live are merely solidified gases; burn them, and they return to their original state, leaving only a hand full of ashes as "material" evidence of their existence, and if we learn to treat these ashes with the right agencies, they, too, will vanish into the ethereal realm. The earth itself, so firm and solid under our feet, was indisputably once a ball of flaming gases and vapors, and in the stage before that, must it not have been still more ethereal? It is all solidified atmosphere. Our own bodies are compounds of gases; in the crematory the human form vanishes. All things came out from the ether, and all things are ether, changed to more or less solid forms by differences in atomic pressure and cohesion.

All this brings us to the conclusion that the many seemingly different substances - iron, wood, coal, lime, water, etc., are merely different forms of one thing; that there is only one elemental substance, from which all created things are shaped. As we find that solid things are the gaseous atmosphere, solidified by an increased atomic pressure, so we shall no doubt find that the gases are produced from one ether, being brought to the semi fluid state by increased pressure, and at last we must conclude that there is one perfectly fluid substance, of which are made all the things which do appear. This One Substance is the stupendous reality behind all the appearances of the material world.

We will now take up the study of this substance. First, we must get rid of the idea that there is anything else. Substance is all there is. We live, and move, and have our being in substance; we, ourselves, are substance. We must conclude that substance cannot have been created, for that it should have been formed out of nothing is unthinkable. Substance always was; forms have been created, and are being continually created, changed, and modified; but the substance of which those forms are made is the same, yesterday and today and forever. When I speak of forms, I mean the so-called "material" universe; suns, stars, planets, seas, continents, trees, plants, gases, and the bodies of animals and men; all these are varying forms of the One Changeless Substance, which is all, and in all. And as this substance has existed through all of time past, so it will exist through all of time future, for it is indestructible; we may change its forms, but not one particle of it can we destroy.

Does this substance occupy all of space? Evidently not, for the more nearly we carry its forms to their original state the more fluid they become; we go from solids back to gases, and from gases to ether, and so on; and we conclude that the one substance must be perfectly fluid, and if that be so, its particles cannot be solidly pressed together; there must be space between them, as in all fluids. Furthermore, if substance filled *all* space motion would be impossible; for substance can only move when there is unoccupied space to move into. And as we know that there is motion, so we know that there must be empty space. This is a matter of some importance when we come to the study of consciousness; for if one substance completely filled all space, it must be absolutely solid, with its atoms pressed rigidly against each other; and not only could there be no motion in any part, but there could be no separate consciousness in any part; if consciousness were possible at all in a perfectly solid substance, it could only be the consciousness of the whole.

But if there is empty space, there is not only room for motion, but there is room for separate portions of substance, which may be conscious within themselves. If there is empty space, there is room for man, as a separate portion of original substance to move about and to have a consciousness of his own. There may be more than one conscious intelligence, though there is only one substance. We close this chapter with the claim that we have demonstrated the existence of three realities; time, space and a substance which moves in space. The next chapter will be devoted to the consideration of consciousness.

Consciousness

That consciousness exists does not need proof; we know, and we know that we know. We are conscious of consciousness; and now we have to consider the source of consciousness. Turning back to the realities we have considered, we find that time cannot be the source of consciousness; we cannot think of time as being conscious, and the same is true of space. We cannot conceive of consciousness as existing in empty space, for there would be nothing there to be conscious; and so we see that only substance can be conscious. Where there is no substance there is nothing, and there can be no consciousness. This is a proposition which you should consider well, until you have mastered it in all its bearings; that there can be no consciousness apart from substance; that empty space cannot be conscious. If consciousness exists - and it does - there is a Conscious Substance.

This point we need to develop very fully, for it is vital. If it is not substance which is conscious, then consciousness must exist in the interstices between the particles of substance, or in empty space; and it is empty space which is conscious, which is unthinkable. But if consciousness exists in substance, then it is the substance itself which is conscious, for there can be nothing in substance but substance. It becomes clear, too, that consciousness cannot be the result of functional action within an organism. Functional action is merely motion, and motion is a shifting of substance from one place to another. If consciousness were produced by motion, would it not still be the substance which was conscious? Try to reason out how a substance could be made conscious by shifting it from one place to another. If consciousness was produced by the motion, then the substance could not have been conscious before it moved, nor could it remain conscious after it ceased to move.

Try to think of a substance as becoming conscious, and endowed with reason, memory and love while making a certain motion, and as losing all these when ceasing to move; try to reason out how motion could come first as a cause, and consciousness follow as a result. Try to conceive of the Original Fluid Substance as beginning, unconsciously, to move; and as producing, unconsciously, all the orderly sequences of forms which appear in nature; and at last, and only at last, becoming fully conscious of it all through the unconscious beginning of a certain motion in the brain of man. Try to think of full consciousness as having been lacking in the universe until certain vibrations were started in the brain of man; you will find all this unthinkable. Consciousness is not the result of motion, but the first cause of motion. It is not motion which is conscious, but substance. The human ego is Conscious Substance.

The next question is whether consciousness is an attribute of substance only in certain forms, or whether it inheres in original fluid substance; and to that we now turn our attention. Is it the brain which is conscious? Those who have kept abreast of the revelations of modern psychology as set forth by William Hanna Thompson and others, know that it is not. The substance of the brain is not conscious; or at least, the substance of the brain is not *the* conscious, thinking, reasoning human ego. We have learned that the brain is the product, rather than the producer of consciousness; and that the intelligent direction of consciousness in the work of brain-building may produce almost any desired change in the structure and capacity of the brain. Furthermore, there are many evidences which go to show that consciousness is not localized in, or confined to the brain, but extends throughout the body; and that we are conscious, not with our brains alone, but with our entire beings. If this should be proved true, and it is likely to be, we will have to conclude that the "physical" body of man is permeated and pervaded by a conscious substance which is co-extensive with it in every part, and which is the real man.

And we must also conclude that this conscious substance is Original Substance, and in a condition approaching its primal state, for it becomes apparent as we go on that complete consciousness can only exist in Original Substance in its primal state. Changes in state and form appear to limit consciousness. The consciousness of the animal creation is limited by their forms and is little, if any, more than sufficient for the reproduction of those forms; the consciousness of the tree and plant is still more limited, but scientists now generally admit that there is consciousness in the vegetable kingdom; and in the mineral world, consciousness appears as directivity of atoms, and chemical affinity. When we come to man, however, we find a capacity for growth in consciousness which seems to be unlimited;

hence we argue that man is Original Substance in its primal state, or at least, that he may attain to the primal state.

Time is; space is. Space is occupied by conscious substance; and there is but one substance, from which are made all the forms of the visible creation. The physical body of man is a form of substance as prepared through the processes of the visible creation; man, himself, is original substance or spirit, inhabiting this physical body. "In the image of God created He them."

It will be seen that while all is God, it is also true that man is man, an independent entity, having a consciousness of his own, and that, while all is spirit, matter exists, being spirit on a varying plane of atomic pressure; and that while it is true that mind is in all and through all, perfect consciousness exists only in original substance, in pure spirit, or in God; and that the nearest approach to complete consciousness is in man, whose unlimited capacity for growth proves him to be at least, a near approach to original substance. We close this chapter with the assertion that time is; that space is, and that space is occupied by a conscious substance which moves. We will next consider the fourth reality: Motion.

Motion

I presume no one will deny that motion is a reality; we know that we move, and we know that motion is going on all around us. The immensity of motion is staggering when we come to consider it; the motions of stars, suns, planets and satellites; of rivers, lakes and seas; of wind and clouds; of the circulation of sap and blood; of atomic vibration, and so on. Motion is the cause of light and heat; of sound, tone, color, electricity, magnetism. Differences in the shape and motion of atoms make bodies solid or gaseous, and differentiate the so-called "substances" from each other. It may be seen then that motion plays an all-important part in the work of creation; that motion is the work of creation in progress; and so the study of motion becomes very important indeed.

What is motion? That which moves is neither time nor space; it is not conceivable that either time or space should move. That which moves is substance. Motion, then, is a shifting of substance from place to place; or from one part of space to another part of space. And are there different kinds of motion? In a way, there are, and the difference depends upon the time used in making the motion, and upon the direction in which the motion is made. That is, there are fast and slow motions; circular and linear motions; and those metaphysicians who contend that time and space do not exist should consider that if there is no time there is no such thing as fast and slow motion; and if there is no space there is no motion at all, for there is no place to move to. No more preposterous absurdity has appeared in modern thought than the denial of the existence of time and space.

Motion, then is the shifting of substance in space and time. And what causes motion? To this you will be ready to answer "forces"; and after a little consideration you will see that that is no answer at all unless you tell what force is. What is force, and how does it cause substance to move? Force is not time; we cannot think of time as causing motion. Force is not space; we cannot think of space as causing motion. If force is substance and causes motion, then substance moves itself; and if force is not substance, then it is nothing, or empty space, and empty space cannot act on substance so as to cause it to move. It is all very well for scientists to write of atoms as being "electrons" or ultimate units of force; but these electrons are either substance or they are not; and if they are not substance they are nothing but empty space, and in that case there is no substance, no existence, no consciousness, no anything. Either force is substance, or it is something in substance; and if it is something in substance which is not substance, what is it? And how can that which has no substance act on substance so us to cause motion? Force is not motion, for it is the cause of motion and the effect cannot be its own cause. Let me now try to give you a definition of Force.

Force is pressure of substance against substance. Try to exert force upon anything in any other way than by pressing substance against it; can you do it? Try to cause a body to move in any other way than by pressing something against it; can you do it? Try to conceive of force as being exerted upon any body without pressing anything against it; try to conceive of force as crossing a complete vacuum where is no substance of any kind. Force is pressure of substance; that it can be anything else is not thinkable.

And this brings us to the consideration of what is loosely spoken of as "attraction". It is stated that all solid bodies "attract" each other, and that every body in the universe attracts every other body; but those who make these assertions do not tell us how the attraction is accomplished. If bodies "attract" each other, then they exert force upon each other; and if they exert force upon each other they must cause pressure upon each other; for how can a body exert force upon another except by causing pressure upon it? If "attraction" is an unsubstantial thing, then it cannot affect substance, or cause motion; if it is an unsubstantial thing, then it is empty space, for where there is no substance there is only empty space. Can you think of an "attraction" crossing an empty space? What would it be like, and how would it get across? Can you think of a "vibration" as crossing an empty space? How would it be transmitted where there was nothing to vibrate? Can you think of a force as crossing an empty space? What would be the shape, size and general appearance of a force apart from substance?

By considering all these points we see that what we know as force is simply pressure of substance; or, one portion of substance pressing against another portion of substance; and that force can be nothing else than this. And we see that pressure causes motion, and that motion, in turn, causes pressure, so that force and motion are mutually convertible, each into the other. Also, we see that there is only one force, the pressure of substance; and that all the so-called "forces" of nature are merely different rates and modes of motion, and have their origin in the One Force - pressure of substance. Furthermore, we see that there is no such thing as a universal attraction which bodies exert upon each other, but that there is a universal pressure, impelling all bodies toward each other in a definite and orderly way; and to the study of this universal pressure we will next turn our attention. Time, space, substance and motion exist. Substance is conscious. Motion is caused by pressure of substance against substance, and the varying forms of substance in the visible creation caused by differences in motion.

The Beginning of Motion

To understand force and motion, we must go back to a supposititious creation. Conceive, first, of space as being occupied by completely conscious substance in a perfectly fluid state, conscious throughout, alike throughout, and without motion. Now, can you conceive of motion as beginning in any part of this substance without an act of will? Can you think of your conscious self as beginning to act, and as continuing to act in an orderly and consecutive series of motions without an effort of will? If, as we have seen, original substance is completely conscious, then its every motion must be a conscious motion; and we cannot think of conscious motion without will. You are aware that you can consciously originate motion yourself; but you cannot do it without will. You are conscious substance; you can be nothing else as we have seen, and you can move or cease to move by an exertion of your will, and in moving or ceasing to move you cause the body you inhabit to move or cease to move. We see motion beginning and ceasing all around us; and we conclude that every motion had a beginning; and that the beginning of the series of creative motions which have resulted in the present universe of forms could only have been in an action of the will of Original Conscious Substance.

In the beginning, then, by an act of will, parts of substance were made to press against each other; and this pressure must pack the substance together, making it more dense, more rigid, and less fluid. This pressure, also, must originate the motions we know as light, heat, electricity and magnetism; and this will-pressure, drawing substance together and holding it in coherent masses, is what we call gravity. It is this will pressure which brings an apple to the earth, and which holds the earth itself in its orbit; which tends to bring all the heavenly bodies together, and which yet holds them apart forever, keeping each in its own place.

There is no accounting for "attraction" on other grounds than that it is the Creative Will of Original Substance, pressing itself together into forms. Every phenomenon of force or motion, from the circling sweep of a planet to the vibration of an atom, has its origin in the will of the great Intelligent Substance to which, or to whom, men have given the name of God. The earth is held together solely by the pressure of the will which permeates it; were that will relaxed, the earth would return instantly to its original fluid condition. Try to think of substance as being held together by something else than will; try to think of substance, originally fluid, as being pressed into solid shapes and held in solid shapes, and going on in orderly and consecutive motions without will; and you will find it unthinkable. The earth is a part of Conscious Being, holding itself in form by the exercise of the will which is in all substance; gravity is the will exerted by substance in pressing itself into form; so also is chemical affinity, or the directivity of atoms. All motion originates in will-pressure. Trace back the motion of the wheels to the engine and thence to the coal; and you say that the latent heat-energy of the coal is causing motion. But what lodged the heat energy in the coal? Was it the will-pressure of gravity, in the distant ages? There is only one force, and that is the will of the Great Intelligence; the eternal creative pressure, moving substance into the various forms in which it appears to us.

In the beginning was God, Spirit, Conscious Substance, occupying the calm deeps of space. An act of will, and there was sufficient pressure to produce the particles of the luminiferous ether, whose vibrations produce light; and there was light. A further act of will, increasing pressing of substance together, and nebulous clouds appear; and by the Great Will these were pressed into spheres with all the accompanying phenomena of the motions of heat and electricity; and so the creation of forms went on until the visible universe appeared as it is; formed of one substance, by the Will of God and maintained and held together by the continued exercise of that Great Will.

The question of motive comes in just here. We cannot conceive of continuous, orderly and systematic action without a motive; and the question must come to our minds, what is the motive of the Great One in His work? With a little reflection, the answer must present itself. He is seeking happiness. We cannot conceive of a conscious being as continuously seeking pain, inharmony or misery. Conscious action can have but one motive, and that motive is ultimate harmony or happiness. The purpose of God in the creation can be nothing else than His own happiness, and since he is All and in All, His happiness can only be attained in the happiness of all. Remember that the purpose of the creation is the happiness of all, including yourself, and that to be unhappy is to oppose the will of the Great Intelligence.

Look now upon the immensity of the visible universe, and contemplate the power of the Creator; see that in all and through all, from the rolling on a planetary system to the rising of the sap in a blade of grass, the one impelling power is the Will of God. And this Great Intelligence is seeking pleasure and happiness in us, and through us. Shall we doubt, then, that He can and will heal our diseases, give us every good thing that we need, and guide us into all truth? In the next chapter, we shall consider man's relation to this Great Intelligence.

Man and His Powers

The universe is a Great Being, who is seeking happiness in and through the forms which he creates from his own substance; and of all these forms, man alone has power to enter into intelligent relations with the Creator. To state it in other words, the great intelligence is seeking happiness in you, and you have power to co-operate intelligently with him in the search. That is what makes you man, the power to work with God in the search for happiness. And if this Great One seeks your happiness, it must be your most permanent and perfect happiness; that is, your highest good; for being conscious of all that there is to be conscious of, and knowing all that there is to know, he is all-wise; and we cannot think of the all-wise as seeking anything less than the highest good, or as being satisfied with anything less than the highest good.

As far as your physical body is concerned, the highest good that can come to you is unquestionably perfect health. The notion that there are circumstances under which pain and sickness are better for man than perfect health must take its place among those superstitious beliefs

99

which have been exploded and discredited. Pain and sickness may be good for man if he takes them rightly, but perfect health is always far better if he takes that rightly; and it is a self-evident proposition that God can find complete delight in man only as man is completely whole. The Great Intelligence, then, seeks perfect health and wholeness in you; and the substance of the Living One, filled with life and power, presses upon you on every side, seeking to impart life and power to you, but you being a portion of that great intelligence, are supreme within your own personality, and so you will have health or not as you receive and recognize this health of God.

If you fail to recognize and receive the All-health, and if you recognize disease within yourself, you prevent God from reaching you; and you form within yourself that which you recognize as existing. If you continuously recognize the perfect health of the Intelligent Substance, in which you live and move and are, and of which you are a part, you cannot be otherwise than well.

It is another self-evident truth that man's highest good demands that he should have the use of all the things he is capable of using in order to live all the life he is capable of living. Man's highest good, and his real happiness can be attained only when he has abundance for every physical and mental need. Just as it is true that God cannot fully delight in you if you are physically sick, so it is true that he cannot find happiness through you if you are mentally or physically starved, or lacking the essentials for life, growth and enjoyment. Happiness consists in living fully; and God can live fully in you only when you have everything to live with. So, the desire of the Great One for you must be that you shall have abundance.

But here again you are supreme within yourself. What if God presses abundance upon you, and you persist in recognizing only privation and poverty? If that be the case, you will remain poor in the midst of abundance, as millions of people are doing; and to be poor, or in want is to oppose the will of God, who seeks happiness in all, and for all. We are parts of himself, and what can he do when his will is opposed and his bounty rejected by a part of himself?

The solution of man's problems of health, wealth, and

growth can be reached when man unifies himself with God, the Great Intelligent Spirit, Substance, who seeks life and happiness in man; and man can unify himself with God only by constantly recognizing God; by considering and acknowledging God, and by looking to God in prayer. The prayer of faith is really an affirmation; and an affirmation is the recognition of an existing fact. When you live in constant and conscious contact with the great intelligent substance you can have no sickness; and his desire for happiness in you will cause the exertion of that mighty will-pressure to bring to you all the things that make for your highest good. The man who can completely unify himself with the divine substance becomes a center toward which the divine will impels every desirable thing; and that man will not, and cannot, lack for anything.

The universe is a Great Being, an intelligent substance, occupying space and using time. His desire leads Him to create forms from His own substance, and in these forms He seeks happiness. Man has but to unify himself with this Great Being to secure the supply of every need, and the gratification of every desire. Man only needs to learn how to pray and how to work.

We Have Book Recommendations for You

The Strangest Secret by Earl Nightingale (Audio CD - Jan 2006)

Acres of Diamonds [MP3 AUDIO] [UNABRIDGED] (Audio CD) by Russell H. Conwell

Automatic Wealth: The Secrets of the Millionaire Mind - Including: Acres of Diamonds, As a Man Thinketh, I Dare you!, The Science of Getting Rich, The Way to Wealth, and Think and Grow Rich [UNABRIDGED] by Napoleon Hill, et al (CD-ROM)

Think and Grow Rich [MP3 AUDIO] [UNABRIDGED] by Napoleon Hill, Jason McCoy (Narrator) (Audio CD - January 30, 2006)

As a Man Thinketh [UNABRIDGED] by James Allen, Jason McCoy (Narrator) (Audio CD)

Your Invisible Power: How to Attain Your Desires by Letting Your Subconscious Mind Work for You [MP3 AUDIO] [UNABRIDGED]

Thought Vibration or the Law of Attraction in the Thought World [MP3 AUDIO] [UNABRIDGED] by William Walker Atkinson, Jason McCoy (Narrator) (Audio CD - July 1, 2005)

The Law of Success Volume I: The Principles of Self-Mastery by Napoleon Hill (Audio CD - Feb 21, 2006)

The Law of Success, Volume I: The Principles of Self-Mastery (Law of Success, Vol. 1) (The Law of Success) by Napoleon Hill (Paperback - Jun 20, 2006)

The Law of Success, Volumes II & III: A Definite Chief Aim & Self -Confidence by Napoleon Hill (Paperback - Jun 20, 2006)

Thought Vibration or the Law of Attraction in the Thought World & Your Invisible Power (Paperback)

Automatic Wealth I, The Secrets of the Millionaire Mind - Including: As a Man Thinketh, The Science of Getting Rich, The Way to Wealth and Think and Grow Rich (Paperback)

The Bestsellers in this Book give sound advice about money and how to obtain it. Just reach for the stars, stay focused on your dreams, and watch them come true. There is nothing we can imagine that we can't do. So what are we waiting for? Let's begin the journey of self-fulfillment.

4 Bestsellers in 1 Book:

As a Man Thinketh by James Allen

The Science of Getting Rich by Wallace D. Wattles

The Way to Wealth by Benjamin Franklin

Think and Grow Rich by Napoleon Hill

BN Publishing

Improving People's Life

www.bnpublishing.com

BN Publishing

Improving People's Life

www.bnpublishing.com

Printed in the United Kingdom
by Lightning Source UK Ltd.
126188UK00001B/33/A